Let's Read

Genesis
and
Exodus

Alan Batchelor

Let's read Genesis and Exodus

This book is dedicated to the dear folk at Lostock Christian Fellowship, Poynton, Cheshire, who have afforded me the privilege of preaching to them on many occasions.

They have patiently listened to my expository sermons and have encouraged me so much with their warm hospitality.

Contents

Preface

Let's read the bible

Genesis

This book is the first in a series, whose aim is to provide a companion as you read for yourself the books of the Bible.

Each book is not a commentary on the books of the Bible, but an aid to clarifying and understanding the contents. While not a commentary, I have included the observations, notes and images from a publication of 1941 entitled "The Bible for today", an edition of the bible edited by John Stirling, with illustrations by Rowland Hilder and other artists.

We are fortunate in these days, thanks to the scholarship of many, to have access to many translations of the Bible and, as Bible readers, we will be drawn to one or more of these versions as our "go to" scripture.

The purpose of this series of books is to encourage everyone to take a fresh look at the Bible and to discover for themselves the insights that it brings to the lives of people in today's world.

It is not the purpose of this series of books to direct you any particular translation of the Bible. Rather it is to invite you to have it alongside you as an aid as you read the Bible in whatever version you choose.

Choose to read a translation of the Bible that you are comfortable with. There are many different versions, from the King James version in 17th century language to modern versions like the New International Version or the Message Bible. It is good, often, to compare passages

May God bless you as we journey together through His Word.

Alan Batchelor, 2023

BUT THE WORD OF THE LORD ENDURETH FOR EVER

Therefore we will not fear, though the earth be changed, the nations rage, and the kingdoms are removed. God's promises are sure, and hsi purposes will be fulfilled

Let's Read

GENESIS

Containing

The Bible's Own Introduction

Beginning of the Good News

The Settler's Story

The Herdsman's Story

The Harvester's story

Genesis

The Name Genesis is Greek, meaning "genealogy," and has been applied to the opening book of the Bible, which begins with the generations (or origins) of the heaven and the earth, and traces from its source the genealogy of the chosen people. In the Hebrew Bible the book bears no title, but is simply indicated by its opening word "In the beginning."

It goes back to the earliest possible commencement, "the beginning," when God created the heavens and the earth; and it indicates at its close that It is the opening of a long history which is to follow. And as the whole Old Testament is the national religious literature of the people of Israel, this first book is obviously intended to trace the history from its source. All the nations of the world that have become historical have asked themselves whence they came, and have given various answers to the question as to the origin of all things. The book of Genesis, looked at by itself, may be regarded as the Scripture answer to such questions. The main purpose is to trace the history of Israel from its source; and to do this the narrative begins with the source of all things.

The book was written for Israelite readers, for the common people, and had to be written in terms which they could understand. It was not written to instruct them in geology or astronomy; so far as it deals ·with the origin of the world, its main purpose is to assert that all things came from God, to start with the lofty view of His almighty power and providence. The book of nature is laid open before man, and he is left by the slow process of reason and research to discover its modes of working. But the knowledge of God Himself is made known to man, and it is the world as made by God and guided and governed by Him that the Bible deals.

THE DAWN LEADS ON ANOTHER DAY

While the earth remaineth, seedtime and harvest, and cold and heat, and summer and winter, and day and night shall not cease.

God has written the name and address of every man on the first page of his book.

Introduction

The Bible is a personal gift. It has a personal message. No other book in the world addresses the reader so directly or speaks to him so intimately and with such deep affection. That is why we cannot look on these opening chapters merely as an introduction to literature or history. They have a more personal character. Just as title-deeds, before they describe the nature of their covenant, give the names of the parties concerned, so these chapters at the beginning of the Bible have been designed to establish the identity of the heir to God's Covenant. Whoever finds himself described there has an indisputable right to all the promises contained in the Book.

The writing is in many ways remarkable. It is in the form of story-pictures: the universal language, the most easily read language, that language which never grows out of fashion, though it is as old as the intelligence of man.

There are three groups of these picture-stories, picture-strips we might call them, for the drawings run in sequence as though they were spelling out a word or building up an idea. The pictures are not in modern style, for they were drawn in the infancy of knowledge. Their outlines are primitive, and some of the details, if we examine them closely, are strange to us. Still, their meaning is clear and easily read.

To get at the significance of these simple stories there is no need to go into all the discussions which have gathered round them. It is wiser to let them first speak for themselves and make their own impression on us. Maybe that is their real purpose, and we shall read them aright, if, as we go over them, we concentrate our attention on the thoughts which instantly leap to our minds.

Take the picture-stories of the Creation. Can any one go

over these and not exclaim, long before he reaches the end, 'Why, I know this world; it is the place where I live; it is my home'? Or take the picture-stories of the Fall of Man. Can any one read these and, as the weaknesses of human nature come into view, refrain from saying, 'I am like that; I have the same thoughts and feelings, the same disposition; I must belong to that family'? It is the same with the stories of the Flood and the Tower of Babel. They open our minds to something more than we actually see in the drawings, just as we read more in a word than its letters. The inner meaning flashes upon us, and we find ourselves thinking not of a world in danger many centuries ago, but of a world in danger to-day. We catch in the stories a likeness to the situation which at present faces mankind, and feel that the Book is a timely as well as a personal gift.

These first impressions are intensified by closer study. We take up the Creation pictures and are astonished at the number of familiar things we see in them. It gradually dawns upon us that what we have here is not merely a declaration that God made the world, but a description of the world He made; in such vivid pictures that we are forced to admit it is our own world we are looking at in this Book of God.

Our Address: This world of ours. The Revelation concerns the world we know.

This world of ours

Read Chapter 1.1 to 2.3

With what familiar touches the truth is brought home to us! How widely known and how close to our doors are the things described! Even a child can recognize them. The sky with its clouds of rain and lamps of light; the land so fertile, so rich with growing seeds and fruitful trees, so full of life that creatures great and small in infinite variety abound in it; are they not always before our eyes? And the sea, teeming with fish and legendary monsters, is it not the same as that which washes our shores and stretches far beyond our horizon? Can we take a walk at any time of day or night and not see this world, and see it as it is described in the sacred narrative, one day one aspect claiming our attention, and another day something else? Today it may be the birds in the trees; tomorrow the brightness of the moon or stars; but there is never a week without a daily scene to remind us of the writing on this page of the Bible.

The tenderest and most effective touch of all, the one feature in the picture-writing which is always speaking to us, but speaking so softly we rarely give heed to it, is the simple common fact of the coming and going of the days. Yet there is no surer indication of the identity of the world we live in with the world of the Sacred Book than this division of time into days with their ever familiar signs of evening and morning. We do not need to go out of doors to see it. Those who are shut up in hospitals, prisons, workshops, and offices, who cannot read the message of the open country, cannot miss it. The chequered pattern of nights and days falls upon all our windows. It is there for all to read, the sign-manual of God.

The Creation

Read chapter 1:1 - 2:3

- Let there be light
- Light separated from darkness
- Day and night –the first day
- The firmament called heaven– the second day
- Earth and seas
  - God called the dry ground "land" and the waters he called "seas"
- Fruit whose seed is in itself
- Let the land produce seed-bearing plants – the third day
- Two great lights and the stars
  - The greater light to govern the day and the lesser light to govern the night – the fourth day
- Living creatures and birds
  - Be fruitful and multiply – the fifth day
- Let the land produce living creatures, livestock and wild animals
- Man in the image of God
- Fill the earth and subdue it

- I give you every green herb for food
- Everything that God had made was very good – the sixth day
- The seventh day blessed and sanctified

Our Name, and our Nature.

The Revelation is for every living soul.

Read Chapter 2.4 to 3.24

There are three pictures of human nature. One shows its good side, one its bad side, and the third the mixture of these two sides in human history.

The first two are portrait studies of a man, the same man, any man. Adam means man. It is not the personal name of the first man, but the common word in the Old Testament for a human being. Obviously the pictures are to be taken together. One is a general sketch of the man in a country-life setting. The other is a 'close-up', an intimate candid portrait, so full of character and expression that we can see the kind of man he is. In both pictures there are features which indicate their antiquity, and details of drawing which in this age would not be attempted, but the main outlines are so true to life we have no difficulty in recognizing the form and nature of an individual like ourselves. We are brought to the tip-toe of personal recognition. But this is the man God made. That is the whole purpose of the drawings.

In what we have called the general sketch there are two plainly marked characteristics of human nature. A man must have something to do and some one to love-a job of work and a woman by his side. It is impossible to look at the picture and not see in these inborn needs of our nature the distinguishing marks of the man God made. They are God-given instincts, to be happy about and proud of. Whoever has them is a child of God. But this fact is perhaps more surely proved by another no less common characteristic which is also shown in the drawing. We are all God-conscious. We may not be conscious of God as our Creator or Father, but we have an ever-present sense of accountability to Him. In every duty we hear His voice. There are times, it is true, when in our duty we think more of the command, especially if it is contrary to our wishes, than of the consciousness of God which it awakens, but in that consciousness lies the hallmark of our identity with the man in this Creation story, and, we may add, the guarantee for all time of the dignity and destiny of our human nature.

Its good side.

Read chapter 2.4 to 2.25

The second creation story

- Man formed of the dust of the earth
- The breath of life

Life in God's Garden

- Man in the Garden of Eden
- The tree of life and the tree of the knowledge of good and evil
- The four rivers
  - Pishon, winds through Havilah, where there is gold
  - Gihon, winds through Cush
  - Tigris, along the east side of Ashur
  - Euphrates
- You are free to eat from any tree in the garden
- But you must not eat of the tree of the knowledge of good and evil
- It is not good for the man to be alone
  - I will make a suitable helper
- Adam names every living creature
- Adam's rib
- "Bone of my bones and flesh of my flesh"
- That is why a man leaves his father and mother and is united to his wife

Its bad side.

Read chapter 3.1 – 24

There are certain things in human nature we wish were not there. They hardly need to be pointed out, but a picture intended to establish our identity must show them. Unfortunately, it is by our disfigurements we are most quickly and surely recognized. They may be physical defects or evil traits of character. In this case, to make identity doubly sure, both are used.

Before we point to these things it is necessary to say a word about the picture itself. So many people look only at the first stage of the drawing. It is, however, more important to look at the finished picture, after the artist has, by many deft touches, completely drawn the figures. We see then what he has been working up to – a life-like portrait of a man and a woman who have had experience of this dark side of human nature and know the distress it brings into human life. It is to them we must look: and it is in them we best see the tell-tale marks of our humanity.

On the physical side, our nature carries the marks of suffering and death. We are not called upon to explain the mysteries but to note the fact. The man God made has, in the course of his life, to suffer pain and face death. How close to him these bitter experiences of life bring us, and how delicately is the feeling which accompanies them that we were not born to die -conveyed in this picture of our common nature.

Our likeness in character to this man is so strong and so humiliating we are almost ashamed to admit it. But this very feeling of shame is contained in the drawing. It is an outstanding characteristic of the God-made man. His shame, and ours, is not of our nature but of our sin. We have by our sin debased our nature. That in itself is enough to make us painfully self-conscious as we look at this portrait, but to fasten the identity more securely upon us the picture-strip traces out the way we sin. Every twist and turn of the path, every excuse we make, every effort we put forward to avoid the consequences of our evil choice; they are all displayed. It is our own heart's story we read, not Adam's; the true and tragic portrait of every man's soul.

The Fall

- The Serpent's question
  - "Did God really say, "you must not eat from any tree in the garden?
- The Woman's reply
  - God did say, "do not eat from the tree in the middle of the garden, or you will die."
- The Serpent:
  - "You will not certainly die"
  - "Your eyes will be opened and you will be like God"
- The woman took and ate and gave some to her husband
- Their eyes were opened and they knew that they were naked
- "Where are you?"
- Adam
  - "The woman you put with me gave me some and I ate"
- The woman
  - "The serpent deceived me"
- To the serpent:
  - "Enmity between you and the woman"
  - "He will crush your head and you will strike his heel"
- To the woman
  - Pain in childbearing
  - Your husband will rule over you
- To Adam
  - Cursed is the ground
  - Dust you are and to dust you will return
- Eve the mother of all living
- Garments of skin
- Banished from the Garden

Its mixed character.

Read chapter 4.1 to 5.32

Every page of human history has the same texture as this chapter: an uneven mixture of good and evil, unfortunately with an excess of evil. Somehow or other evil always seems to get more than its share of attention. It does so here. The references to anything good are very few. But the point is not so much the unevenness of the mixture as the closeness of the yarn. At the outset we are told that Cain and Abel are brothers. Good and evil are as close together in human life as members of the same household. Closer even than this. For they are found together in a man's heart. Cain, evil as he was, had some goodness in him.

Take a wider view, says the story, and you will observe in the fabric of civilization the same material and the same interweaving. On the one hand, you have Lamech and his sons singing the Song of the Sword – a proud, boastful war song – and on the other, the sons of Seth calling upon the name of the Lord. The war song is more popular. Tribesmen can be heard singing it, workers in brass and iron keeping time to it, and musicians devising variations of it. Both are there, the war song and the hymn of worship.

In the world at large, in the family, in the hearts of men, in human nature generally, says the narrative, there is good and evil. A commonplace truth, but it is by these obvious and easily read signs the Book of God makes homely people feel it has been written about them and must have been written for them.

Cain and Abel

Read chapter 4:1-16

- Birth of Cain and Abel
- Abel kept flocks, Cain worked the soil
- Cain's offering
- Abel's offering - fat portions
- Cain's anger, sin is lying at the door
- Cain killed Abel
- "Where is your brother?"
  - "Am I my brother's keeper?"
- Cain, a restless wanderer

- A mark on Cain
- Cain went out from the Lord's presence

Cain's children

Read chapter 4: 17-18

- Enoch
  - Irad
    - Mehujael, the father of Methushael, the father of Lamech

Lamech and his family

Read chapter 4: 19-24

- Lamech's two wives, Adah and Zillah
- Adah's son– Jabal, raised livestock
- Zillah's sons
  - Jubal, player of instruments and pipes
  - Tubal-Cain, maker of tools
  - daughter Naamah
- Lamech's boast: I have killed a man for wounding me

The birth of Seth

Read chapter 4: 25-26

- God has granted me another child in place of Abel

Generations of Adam

Read chapter 5: 1-20

- Adam, 930 years, had Seth and other sons and daughters
- Seth, 912 years, had Enosh and other sons an daughters
- Enosh, 905 years, had Kenan and other sons and daughters
- Kenan, 910 years, had Mahalel and other sons and daughters
- Mahalel, 895 years, had Jared and other sons and daughters

- Jared, 962 years, had Enoch and other sons and daughters

Enoch and Methuselah
Read chapter 5: 21-31

- Enoch, 365 years, had Methuselah and other sons and daughters
- Enoch walked faithfully with God 300 years: then he was no more for God took him
- Methuselah, 969 years, had Lamech and other sons and daughters
- Lamech, 777 years, had Noah and other sons and daughters

Noah
Read chapter 5:32

- After 500 years had Shem, Ham and Japheth

Our own times: The Spirit of the Age.

The Revelation is for times like these.

Read Chapters 6.1 to 10.32

How far from modern times some of the Bible stories take us! We wonder what value they can have at this long distance for people who are perplexed and hard pressed by a very different form of civilization. Then suddenly in the far-off scene we catch some feature which seems familiar to our experience. It lights up the whole page, and things which we thought had nothing in common with our present existence begin to remind us strangely of what we have read in our daily newspapers.

There is the same kind of material. The emphasis is different, but the facts which are recorded are the usual items of human interest in any and every age. Popular heroes, political and social events, outbreaks of violence, and achievements in sport are not new features of the modern daily press. They are all mentioned in this sacred chronicle of the world's news; they are part of the day's story in every era. We are, however, so keen to get the latest news of our own time that we do not often look at this old-time picture. If we did we might get a better perspective of our own civilization. For the truth is we have in this Bible picture something more than the signs of the times. We have the spirit of the times, and the nearer we get to it the stronger grows our conviction that it is not the spirit of bygone times, but of our own times, of all times, which we see on these immortal pages.

We see the eyes of the people looking with hope and fear to the giants of their generation –'demigods' the ancient text naively calls them, because they seem to possess superhuman gifts. We see the pride in military conquests which bring territorial gains, and the ambition which seeks its own glory in pretentious social schemes. We see, too, outrages which shock the moral sense, and the bold effrontery of anti-God campaigns. Whether we look in the Bible or at our newspapers these are the signs of the spirit of the age.

What, however, the newspapers do not say, the story of the Flood boldly proclaims. There is a moral as well as a social order in the world, a Divine as well as a natural order in the universe, and woe betide that civilization which is blind to it. But-and this in the Bible is front-page news-the man who keeps the faith in a faithless age is in God's care.

At the time of the flood

Read chapter 6: 1-8

- Human beings increased in number
- Limited to 120 years
- Giants in those days
- Wickedness of the human race
- The Lord's heart deeply troubled
- "I will destroy man whom I have created
- Noah found favour in the eyes of the Lord

The Ark

Read chapter 6: 9-22

- Noah - a righteous man
- "I am going to put an end to all people"
- An ark of Cypress wood

- Its details
- Warning of a flood
- "I will establish my covenant with you
- Two of all living creatures
- Noah's obedience
- Noah and his family enter the ark

The Deluge

Read chapter 7:1-8:5

- Noah, his wife, his sons and their wives
- Pairs of all creatures, to keep their various kinds alive throughout the earth
- The Lord shut him in
- Forty days
- Waters rose and covered the mountains
- Everything that had the breath of life died
- The Earth flooded for a hundred and fifty days
- Water receded steadily
- Ark rested on the Mountains of Ararat
- Tops of the mountains visible in the tenth month

The Raven and the Dove

Read chapter 8: 1-19

-
- After forty days Noah sent out a raven
- Raven flying back and forth
- Dove sent out, but returned
- After seven days, the dove with an olive leaf
- Twenty seventh day of the second month the earth was dry
- Come out of the ark; bring out every creature that is with you

The Altar

Burnt offerings

Read chapter 8; 20-22

- Noah sacrificed burnt offerings
- "never again will I curse the ground because of humans."
- "As long as the earth endures, seedtime and harvest, cold and heat, summer and winter, day and night will never cease."

God's covenant with Noah. The Blessing

Read chapter 9; 1-17

- Be fruitful and increase in number and fill the earth
- I now give you everything
  - but you must not eat meat that has its lifeblood still in it
- For your lifeblood I will demand an accounting
- "Whoever sheds human blood, by humans shall their blood be shed."

The Rainbow

- I establish my covenant with you
  - Never again will all life be destroyed by the waters of a flood
- The sign of the covenant

The Curse of Canaan

Read chapter 9: 18-28

- Noah planted a vineyard
- Noah lay drunk and uncovered
  - Seen by Ham, the father of Canaan
- Shem and Japheth walked backwards and covered their father
- When Noah awoke

- Cursed be Canaan! The lowest of slaves will he be to his brothers
- May Canaan b e the slave of Shem
- May Canaan be the slave of Japheth
- Noah lived 950 years, and then he died

Sons of Noah

Read chapter 10: 1-32

- Sons of Japheth
  - Gomer, Magog, Madai, Javan, Tubal, Meshek, Tiras
    - Sons of Gomer: Ashkenaz, Riphath, Togarmah
  - Sons of Javan
    - Elisha, Tarshish, the Kittites, the Ridanites
    - from these the maritime peoples spread out
- Sons of Ham
  - Cush, Egypt, Put, Canaan
    - Sons of Cush: Seba, Havilah, Sabtah, Raamah, Sabteka
    - Sons of Raamah: Sheba, Dedan
- Cush was the father of Nimrod, a mighty warrior, a mighty hunter
  - The centres of his kingdom: Babylon, Uruk, Akkad, Kalneh, Shinar
  - He built Nineveh, Rehoboth Ir, Calah, Resen
- Egypt was the father of the Ludites, Anamites, Lehabites, Naphtuhites, Pathrusites, Kasluhites, caphtoritres
- Canaan was the father of Sidon, the Hittites, Jebusites, Amorites, Girgashites, Hivites, Arkites, Sinites, Arvadites, Zemarites, Hamathites
  - the borders of Canaan reached from Sidon to Gaza, then toward Sodom and Gomorrah as far as Lasha
- Sons of Shem
  - Elam, Ashur, Arphaxad, Lud, Aram
  - Sons of Aram: Uz, Hul, Gether, Meshek
  - Arphaxac was the father of Shelah, the father of Eber

- Eber had two sons: Peleg, Joktan
  - Joktan's sons: Almodad, Sheleph, Hazarmaveth, Jerah, Hadoram, Uzal, Diklah, Obal, Abimael, Sheba, Ophir, Havilah, Jobab
- From these the nations spread out over the earth after the flood

The Tower of Babel.

Read Chapter 11 1-22

How close it stands to present-day schemes of self-defence—a monument, which Time cannot utterly destroy, to all our foolish boasts of self-sufficiency. On more and more ambitious lines the same vain work goes on. Iron and steel reinforce the bricks and mortar of the early days. The tower which rose high to the sky now runs to the sea like a wall fortified with battlements and battalions. Fear of man has been added to the fear of God. In the hearts of men there is widespread alarm that the world may again be devastated as it was at the Flood or in the Great War. At all costs, these ardent workers say, we must make ourselves safe, and we will do so on such a scale that throughout the world our name will be exalted. Is not this the spirit of the age? It is the spirit of this page of Scripture, and makes the Bible a book for our own times, with to-day's date written in it.

When we get to the heart of these stories of Genesis we find, to our amazement, that we are at the heart of all things—of the world in which we live, of the mysteries of our own being, and of the problems which beset every age of human existence. Scripture is the script of life. Once we have become familiar with the picture-form of writing, it is easy to read the whole Book. For it is a book of pictures, pictures of everyday life: waiting, not to be interpreted, but to be recognized, and to impart at the moment of recognition the revelation which the pictures carry. This great story of Revelation begins with Abraham. The lives of his children and their descendants are the pages on which it is written. But the story is for you and me, and these introductory chapters of Genesis, stamped with today's date and bearing our address and portrait, convey it to us.

Read chapter 11: 1-9

- One language and a common speech
- A plain in Shinar
- Build a city with a tower that reaches to the heavens
- Make a name for ourselves
- Language confounded
- Scattered over all the earth

From Shem to Abram

Read chapter 11: 10-

- Arphaxad
- Shelah
- Eber
- Peleg
- Reu
- Serug
- Nahor
- Terah
- Abram

Terah's family line

Read chapter 11: 27-32

- Terah's sons: Abram, Nahor, Haran
  - Haran was the father of Lot, died in Ur of the Chaldeans
  - Abram's wife was Sarai
  - Sarai was childless
  - Nahor's wife was Milkah
- Terah and his family went from Ur to Harran
- Terah died in Harran

Holy Land:

In the land of Revelation we see the Revelation for all lands

THE LAND CHOSEN FOR THE DIVINE REVELATION

The country we call Palestine, the original home of the Israelites, is about the size of Wales. On maps of the ancient world it occupied a central position, and formed a natural stage on which to set before the eyes of all men the Revelation of God.

To the hills and fields of our own pleasant land comes the revelation of this book of God

Beginning of the Good News

Our earliest record is the life-history of the man who was called God's Friend

Read Chapter 12.1 to 14.24

Look not, says Abraham, for the story of my life in these chapters, but for the story of my God. There is none like Him. And this is His glory; He has come forward, not with a scheme merely, but with a promise for the world, and a promise which is more wonderful than anything the mind of man could possibly have conceived. More than that; He has pledged Himself to see it fulfilled. This is the never-to-be-forgotten message, the news from heaven, which we are to pass on to the children of men in all generations.

And with the news pass on my own heart's witness to its truth. For I have known Him of whom I speak, intimately, and this one fact He has, through all my length of days, brought me to believe: that He can be known and loved and trusted as a personal friend. Friend, did I say, while I speak of God? It is the name my heart, if not my lips, must utter. For, of all the gods, if there are a any beside Him, He alone has been my Friend. To me there is no other in earth or heaven; no other Living God; no other God, who speaks to man, who walks with him, through all the years of his earthly pilgrimage, that man might learn, in fellowship with Him, the ways of righteousness and peace.

There is one God in all the earth. The Call of Abraham

Read chapter 12: 1-9

- Go from your country to a land that I will show you
- I will make you into a great nation
- All peoples on earth will be blessed through you
- Abram went, as the Lord had told him
- Abram was seventy-five years old
- To your offspring I will giv e this land
- Abram built an altar and called on the name of the Lord

Note on 12:3 There are two ways of reading this passage. Abraham will be an instrument of blessing, or such an example of blessedness that others will seek the Divine favour

In Egypt
Read chapter 12: 10-20

- Famine in the land
- Abram's deception: "Say you are my sister."
- Abram treated well for her sake
- Serious deseases inflicted on Pharaoh and his household
- "Here is your wife. Take her and go."

Note on 12.17 God cares for Abraham's wife as well as for Abraham. Although Abraham falls short of his duty, God does not cast him off

In the Hill Country
Read chapter 13: 1-4

- Abram, wealthy in livestock, silver and gold
- From place to place
- Between Bethel and Ai
- Called on the name of the Lord

On the Plains. Abram and Lot separate
Read chapter 13: 5-18

- Lot also had herds and tents
- Quarreling among the herders
- Abram offered a choice to Lot
- Lot chose the whole plain of the Jordan
- Parting company
- Lot near Sodom
- The wickedness of Sodom
- God's promise to Abram:
  - All the land that you see I will give to you and your offspring forever.
  - I will make your offspring like the dust of the earth

It is impossible for anyone to visit the Holy Land and not see on the hill and in the fields something which reminds him of his own country. And this is true from whatever country he comes. For the natural features of Palestine are such that animals and plants native to every zone are, or have been, found there. In this representative strip

of country, this characteristic sample of the earth, the Revelation of God was given to show that every land is a Holy Land. 'Holy' in the same sense that Canaan was holy; because God was in it. He who made himself known in Canaan has since those days revealed his presence in every part of the earth.

- Abram went to live at Hebron

Note on chapter 14 In this section Abraham is a valiant warrior. It may be, some think, an inserted story. It is more than likely that the original narrative, as it passed through different periods of history, was drawn out to suit the needs of the times. Prophets, priests, patriots, have all, doubtless worked upon it. We are privileged to look at the finished picture, and it is not Abraham, but Abraham's God who claims our attention.

- Kings at war
- Four kings against five
- Tar pits in the Valley of Siddim
- The four kings seized all the goods of Sodom and Gomorrah
- Lot taken captive
- Abram assembled 318 trained men and went in pursuit
- Rescue of Lot and his possessions
- Melchizedek, King of Salem and priest of God brought out bread and wine and blessed Abram
- Abram gives tithes to Melchizedek
- Abram accepts nothing from the King of Sodom

Note on chapter 14 v 18: Salem later became known as Um-Salem, or Jerusalem, 'the city of peace', and this city of a beautiful name has become known to the world as the City of God. Coming out of it we see the king of peace (Salem), 'the priest of the most high God', with gifts in his hands and blessing on his lips for the man who has put his trust in God. It would indeed be surprising if an incident of this character and description did not become invested with symbolic significance The marvel is that it should appear at this point of the story. The writer to the Hebrews specifically mentions this priest Melchizedek in chapter 7

The God of Nature is the God of Nations

Read chapter 15.1 to 20.18

He is the God of all the peoples of the earth. Ishmael, Lot, and

Abimelech are not outside His care. Sodom and Gomorrah are not beyond His visitation. But we can hardly look upon these persons or the inhabitants of these cities as the people of God. Yet they were in the land of God. So God spoke to Abraham, saying, I will give you a son, and make you a nation, and My land shall be filled with people after My own heart. This is the meaning of the promise, and of the covenant, described here, which provides for the consecration of all children born to Abraham and his descendants. There shall be a new race, a better nation, or, as later developments revealed, a new community, countless as the stars, which will fill the earth and be known as the people of God.

The Lord's Covenant with Abram

Read chapter 15: 1-20

- I am your shield and very great reward
- Abram's complaint that he is childless
- The Lord promises a son
- Abram believed the Lord, and he credited it to him as righteousness
- The Heifer, a goat, a ram, a dove, a young pigeon
- Abram's deep sleep
- Prophecy about the slavery
  - For four hundred years your descendants will be strangers in a country not their own and they will be enslaved
  - I will punish the nation they serve as slaves
  - Your descendants will come back here
- The Lord's covenant with Abram
  - To your descendants I give this land

Note on 15:17 The Covenant made with Abraham has the features of a royal investiture, which bestows an estate or office upon a subject, and betokens the close relationship between the parties. The installation is a solemn ceremony, and includes conferring a new name or title upon the subject, who swears allegiance and loyal service to his king. Often the honour conferred and the estate bestowed pass as an inheritance to his son, and his descendants.

Stonehenge on Salisbury Plain, Wiltshire, was once an open-air altar

The Birth of Ishmael

Read chapter 16: 1-16

- Sarai's handmaid given to Abram as a wife
- Sarai's regret: "You are responsible for the wrong I am suffering."
- Hagar despised her mistress and is sent away
- The angel and the prophecy concerning Ishmael
  - He will live in hostility toward all his brothers
- "You are the God who sees me"
- Ishmael is born when Abram was eighty six years old

The Covenant of Circumcision and Consecration of Children

Read chapter 17: 1-27

- Abram at ninety-nine years old
- Walk before me faithfully and be blameless
- You will be the father of many nations
- Your name will be Abraham
- I will establish my everlasting covenant with you and your descendants
- Every male to be circumcised; it will be the sign of the covenant between me and you
- Any uncircumcised male will be cut off from my people
- Sarai will be called Sarah
- She will be the mother of nations

- Abraham's doubt; will a son be born to a man a hundred years old?
- Sarah will bear a son and you will call him Isaac
- Ishmael will be the father of twelve rulers
- Every male in Abraham's household was circumcised

The Promise of a son

Read chapter 18:1-15

- The three visitors
- Abraham's hospitality
- "Your wife will have a son next year
- Sarah's laughter
    - Will I really have a child, now that I am old?
- Is anything too hard for the Lord

Note on 18:2 Attempts to explain this naive description raise more difficulty than they remove. At some point in the conversation Abraham realised that God was speaking to him in the words of one of the visitors. The same thing happens today.

Abraham pleads for the righteous of Sodom and Gomorrah

Read chapter 18:16 - 33

- "Shall I hide Abraham from what I am about to do?"
- The sin of Sodom and Gomorrah
    - "Will you sweep away the righteous with the wicked?"
    - "What if there are fifty righteous people?"
    - "What if there are five less than fifty righteous people?"
    - "What if only forty are found there?"
    - "What if only thirty can be found there?"
    - "What if only twenty can be found there?"
    - "What if only ten can be found there?"
    - "For the sake of ten, I will not destroy it."

Sodom and Gomorrah destroyed

Fire from heaven is, of course, a primitive description of lightning

Read chapter 19: 1-29

- Lot invites the Angels to stay
- His house surrounded
- Lot offers his daughters
- Lot under pressure
- Men outside struck with blindness
- Lot urged to flee with his family
- Don't look back and don't stop in the plain
- Lot flees to Zoar
- Burning sulfur on Sodom and Gomorrah
- Lot's wife looked back, and she became a pillar of salt

Lot and his family

Read chapter 19: 30-38

- Living in a cave
- His daughters' plan. There is no man to give us children
  - Preserve our family line through our father
- Both daughters pregnant by their father
- The older daughter had a son, named Moab
  - He is the father of the Moabites
- The younger daughter had a son named Ben-Ammi.
- He is the father of the Ammonites

A Nation spared

Read chapter 20: 1-18

- Abraham in Gerar

- Sarah is my sister
- God speaks to Abimelek in a dream
- Abimelek's clear conscience
- Abraham's reason
- Abraham's instruction to Sarah
- Abimelek's gift to Abraham
- The Lord heals Abimelek, his wife and female slaves

Sovereign Lord and Lover of Mankind.

Read Chapter 21.1 to 23.20

How else can we interpret this section which combines absolute decrees and deeds of infinite compassion? The powers of life and death are in the hands of this Almighty God, but love is there, too, and children must not be offered in sacrifice to Him. It is only when we know God by these names of Lord and Love that we can understand the story of the sacrifice of Isaac, or receive it as a revelation of His glory.

Birth of Isaac

Read chapter 21:1-13

- God fulfils his promise
- "God has brought me laughter."
- "Get rid of that slave woman and her son."
- "Through Isaac your offspring will be reckoned."
- "I will make the son ot the slave into a nation also."

Hagar and Ishmael

Read chapter 21: 14-21

- Hagar and Ishmael in the wilderness
- "Do not be afraid. Lift the boy up, for I will make him into a great nation."
- The well of water
- A wife for him from Egypt

Abimelek's Testimony

Read chapter 21: 22-34

- Abraham's oath to Abimelek
- Complaint over a well
- Abraham's treaty with Abimelek at Beersheba
- Seven ewe lambs as a witness that Abraham dug the well
- Abraham stayed in the land of the Philistines for a long time

Offering of Isaac

Read chapter 22: 1-19

- God tests Abraham
- Sacrifice your son as a burnt offering
- Abraham's obedience
- "Where is the lamb for the burnt offering?"
- "God himself will provide the lambAbraham builds an altar
- "Do not lay a hand on the boy."
- The ram caught in a thicket
- Jehovah Jireh - The Lord will provide
- Through your offspring all nations on earth will be blessed, because you have obeyed me

Note on chapter 22:10

A terrible custom was in vogue and had to be abrogated. So God made it clear to Abraham that child sacrifices were not to be made to Him. This meant new thoughts of God for Abraham. It is difficult for us, who have been brought up in the knowledge of the Fatherhood of God, to realize the overwhelming amazement of a man who has suddenly and unexpectedly been made aware of the father-heart of the Almighty, by a token of tender care for his own son. It is impossible to measure the significance or the far-reaching results of such a moving revelation and experience.

Relatives of Abraham

Read chapter 22: 20-24

- Abraham's brother Nahor's children
  - Uz, Buz, Kemuel, Kesed, Hazo. Pildash, Jidlaph, Bethuel
  - Bethuel became the father of Rebekah
- Nahor's concubine Reumah also had sons:
  - Tebah, Gaham, Tahash, Maakah

Death of Sarah

Read chapter 23:1-20

- Sarah, 127 years old
- Abraham buys a plot from the Hittites
- The field and the cave of Machpelah
- Bought for 400 shekel's of silver
- Sarah is buried

Note on 23:17 Abraham bought all the rights. The text is in the form of a legal contract on which everything is specified.

THE SETTLER'S STORY

The Settler's Story

It reads like a fireside tale told to the family circle, but it contains news of God for every home

Read Chapter 24.1 to 28.9

The God of Nations is the God of the Family. That is the great truth, says Isaac, which this age of revelation has impressed upon me. I had the first hint of it when I went with my father to the mount of sacrifice, but it was not until I had a home of my own that the full glory of the fact took possession of my heart. My home was like many others, where children and aged relatives make up the family circle. Intrigues and quarrels sometimes arose, and the shadow of death fell upon our rejoicings. But this I found: God was in the home as well as in the country.

Isaac and Rebekah

Read chapter 24: 1-67

- Abraham's servant entrusted to go to Abraham's native land to get a wife for Isaac
- The Lord will send his angel before you
- The well outside the town, when the women go out to draw water
- The servant's prayer
- Rebekah: "I will draw water for your camels, too."
- The nose ring and the bracelets
- The Servant: "The Lord has led me on the journey."
- Rebekah's brother Laban
- Come, you who are blessed by the Lord
- The servant states his commission from Abraham
- The marriage is agreed
- The journey home
- Rebekah and Isaac meet.
- He married Rebekah and was comforted after his mother's death.

Note on Chapter 24:53

The gifts to Rebekah formed the bridegroom's gift to the bride; those to the mother and brother the price paid to the family for the bride.

The death of Abraham

Read chapter 25; 1-11

- Abraham's new wife Keturah and her sons
  - Zimran, Jokshan, Medan, Midian, Ishbak, Shuah
- Abraham gave gifts to these sons and sent them away
- Abraham left everything he owned to Isaac
- Abraham lived a hundred and seventy five years andbreathed his last
- Buried in the cave of Machpelah by Isaac and Ishmael

The sons of Ishmael

Read chapter 25: 12 - 18, also recorded in 1 Chronicles 1: 29-31

- Nebaioth, Kedar, Adbeel, Mibsam, Mishma, Dumah, Massa, Hadad, tema, Jetur, Naphish, Kedemah
- They were 12 tribal rulers
- Ishmael lioved a hundred and thurty seven years
- His descendants lived in hostility to all the tribes related to them

Jacob and Esau.

Read chapter 25: 19-34

- Rebekah was childless
- Jacob's prayer
- "Two nations are in your womb."
- The older will serve the younger
- Esau, like a hairy garment
- Jacob, grasping Esau's heel
- Esau, a skilful hunter
- Jacob, a plain man, dwelling in tents

The Family Birthright

- Isaac loved Esau, but Rebekah loved Jacob
- A bowl of stew in exchange for the birthright.
- So Esau despised his birthright

Note on 25:31 The firstborn had the right to a double portion of the property

A New Home.

Read chapter 26:1-16

- Famine
- Isaac went to Abimelek king of the Philistines
- "Do not go down to Egypt"
- Covenant reaffirmed
- Isaac stayed in Gerar

In the days of Esau, hunting was a necessity

- Isaac deception concerning Rebekah
  - She is my sister
- Abimelek's order
  - Anyone who harms this man or his wife shall be put to death
- Isaac blessed by God
- The Philistines stopped up the wells.

Jealous Servants.

Read chapter 26: 17-32

- Isaac reopens the wells in the Valley of Gerar
- Servants quarrel over new wells
- The Lord appears to Isaac at Beersheba
  - Do not be afraid, for I am with you.
- Relations with Abimelek restored

Jacob takes Esau's blessing.

Read chapter 26: 34 - 28:9

Note: The blessing, in addition to blessing the land, which was the birthright Jacob had 'purchased' from Esau, gave him the right of lordship over his brother.

- Esau's Wives: A source of grief to Isaac and Rebekah
- Isaac prepares to give his blessing

- Rebekah's plan to deceive
- Jacob's doubt
- The plan enacted
- Jacob's deceit
  - I am Esau, your firstborn.
- Isaac's blessing
  - May nations serve you
  - Be lord over your brothers
  - May those who curse you be cursed, and those who bless you be blessed
- Esau's return
  - Your brother came deceitfully, and took your blessing
- "Bless me too, my father
- "You will live by the sword and you will serve your brother
- Esau's hatred of Jacob
- Advice to flee to Rebekah's brother Laban in Haran
- "Do not marry a Canaanite woman
- Jacob sent to Paddan Aram
- Esau marries Mahalath, another Canaanite woman

The Herdsman's Story

Thrilling news of a plain man's discovery in the everyday struggle for existence.

Read Chapter 28.10 to 36.43

Write down this news, says Jacob, where all the sons of men can read it; publish it in the streets and market-places, in the fields and on the highways-the God who is over all the earth and all its peoples is the personal God of every individual. Of the man who has done wrong? Look at me, the crafty, deceitful thief and fugitive, ashamed as I am now to own it. Yet He found me, spoke to me, blessed me. Where is the man He has not blessed more than he deserves? But the plain man, the man on the road, the hired labourer in the fields, is the Great God mindful of him? Is not that just how and where He found me? I tell you He is close to everyone. And when trouble comes, as it came to me in my later years, trouble almost too heavy to be borne, because it was brought upon me by my own children, His help fails not.

On the Road

- Jacob's dream at Bethel
- A stairway to Heaven
- God's promise to Jacob
- Jacob's response

Rachel, the Shepherdess.

Read chapter 29

- The well near Haran
- Watering his uncle's sheep
- Jacob greets Rachel
- Laban's welcome
- Working for Laban
- Seven Years for Rachel
- Laban's deceit
- A further seven years

- Leah's children
  - Reuben
  - Simeon
  - Levi
  - Judah

Note on 29.18: This service without pay was instead of the customary price paid for a bride. When he found out that he had been deceived and had to serve another seven years, it is to his credit that he kept the bargain.

Jacob's family increases.

Read chapter 30:1-24

- Bilhah's children
  - Dan
  - Naphtali
- Zilpah's children
  - Gad
  - Asher
- Reuben's mandrakes
- More children for Leah
  - Issachar
  - Zebulun
  - Dinah
- The birth of Joseph

Note on 30:14 Mandrake: a plant having purple flowers, yellow fruits and a forked root; possibly used as an aphrodisiac. A root that was believed to increase fertility.

Jacob's flocks increase.

Read chapter 30: 25-43

- Jacob's desire to return to his homeland
- Laban's answer
- Jacob's proposal about the flocks
- Weak animals to Laban, stronger animals to Jacob
- Jacob becomes prosperous

The shepherd in the east is the brother of all shepherds.

Homeward Bound.

Read chapter 31: 1-19

- Laban's change toward Jacob
- Jacob's informs Rachel and Leah that Laban has cheated him
- Jacob's dream
- "Leave this land"
- Rachel and Leah's reply
- Jacob's departure
- Rachel steals her father's household gods

Laban pursues Jacob.

Read chapter 31: 20-42

- Laban's dream
- "Why did you steal my gods?"
- Jacob's rash words
- The search for the household gods
- Jacob recounts his twenty years with Laban

Note on 31:19 These household gods or images, like the mascots which superstitious people treasure today, were supposed to bring luck. Jacob did not believe in them, and later told his household to get rid of them.

The Boundary Stone.

Read 31: 43 - 55

- Heap of stones set up to mark a boundary between Jacob and Laban
- Laban returns home

Nearing Home.

Read 32: 1-21

- Messenger sent to Esau
- Esau coming to meet Jacob with four hundred men
- Jacob's fear and his prayer
- A gift for his brother

An All-night Struggle.

Read chapter 32: 22-32

- Crossing the Jabbok
- Wrestling with a man till daybreak
- Jacob's name changed to Israel
- "I saw God face to face"

Note on 32.22-32: When Jacob thought he was alone, he discovered he was not alone. There was a mysterious someone, mightier than himself with him, taking hold of him. He struggled to get free, and in the effort realized it was Living God he was fighting against. The moment the truth flashed upon him, he tightened his grasp, refused to let Him go as the dawn drew near. With a day of danger and difficulty before him he cried, 'I will not let Thee go, except Thou bless me'.

Welcome Home.

Read chapter 33:1-17

- Jacob prepares to meet Esau
- Esau's greeting
- Esau accepts Jacob's gift
- Esau returns to Seir but Jacob goes to Succoth

Days of Distress.

Read chapter 33:18 -34:31

- Jacob buys a plot of ground
- Dinah is raped
- The response of Jacob's sons
- Hamor's plea
- Shechem's request
- The deceit of Jacob's sons
- Circumcision of all the males
- Simeon and Levi's attack
- "You have brought trouble on me"

Note on chapter 34. If the first half of Jacob's life shows that blessings come to an evil man, the second part shows that trials come to a good man

Jacob's God.

Read chapter 35:1-15

- Get rid of your foreign gods
- An altar at Bethel
- "your name will be Israel."
- God's promise.

Note on 35:14 It will be remembered that Jacob poured oil on the stone he used for a pillow, when he dreamed of a heavenly ladder. This altar may have been the fulfilment of a vow he then made.

Deaths of Rachel and Isaac.

Read chapter 35:16-29

- Rachel dies giving birth to Benjamin
- Reuben slept with Bilhah
- Jacob's twelve sons
- Isaac died at Mamre

Esau's descendants.

Read chapter 36

Esau's wives and children
- Adah
  - Elephaz
    - Teman, Omar, Zepho, Gatam, Kenaz, + Amelek
- Oholibamah
  - Jeush,Jalam, Korah
- Basemath
  - Reuel
    - Nahath, Zerah, Shammah, Mizzah
- The sons of Seir the Horite
- The kings who reigned in Edom before any Israelite king
- The chiefs descended from Esau

Every harvest field draws our eyes to the Bible Story

The Harvester's Story:

Dreams come true as God's purpose ripens and his promises to mankind are fulfilled.

Read Chapter 37.1 to 50 26

In my life, says Joseph, I have seen the God of Nature and of Nations declare His Sovereignty in lands far from my home and among people mightier than my own. His Love, too, I have seen, as Isaac and Jacob saw it, overshadowing the Family Circle and the personal lives of men. But more than this has been made manifest to me, God has declared Himself to be not only the God of the patriarchs, Abraham, Isaac, and Jacob, but the God also of youth, of young people; even those who, like me, have suffered the loss of home and friends and fortune, and have had nothing left to them in the world but their youth and their dreams. Now I know, His care covers them, His Covenant claims them, and, with their loyalty and devotion, He will bring to pass before the eyes of the world all He has purposed in His heart to do for mankind. So, to you, the youth of all generations I speak; for on you the bright light of this revelation falls.

Joseph and his Dreams.

Read chapter 37:1-11

- Joseph's report on his brothers
- A coat of many colours
- His first dream
- His second dream
- The jealousy of his brothers

Joseph sold by his Brothers.

Read chapter 37:12-36

- Grazing the flocks
- Joseph's errand
- The plot to kill him
- The caravan of Ishmaelites
- Twenty shekels of silver
- Jacob mourns
- Sold to Potiphar in Egypt

Note: When did this happen? Can we fix the date? Only approximately, though we feel in the story of Joseph we are getting on to more solid ground than is provided by the earlier narratives of Genesis. The general view is that Joseph was taken to Egypt during the reign of one of the Shepherd-Kings, who formed the Hyksos dynasty. They were Asiatic invaders who had conquered the Egyptians, and ruled over the country for about 500 years. Authorities differ as to the length of the Hyksos domination.

Judah and Tamar.

Read chapter 38

- Judah's wife and children
- Tamar, a wife for Judah's son Er
- Deaths of Er and Onan
- Tamar in her father's household
- Tamar's disguise
- Judah's sin

- Judah's pledge
- Tamar pregnant
- "She is more righteous than I."
- The scarlet thread
- Birth of Perez and Zerah

Note on Chapter 38: Apparently, in the tribe of Judah, there were a number of semi-foreign clans, and one of the objects of this page was to explain their origin. It was also intended to support an old custom or law concerning widows, which at one time was in force among many races but has long since been abandoned. If two brothers shared an estate and one died without leaving a son, his widow must not, according to this institution, marry into another family, but must marry the surviving brother and bear a son to inherit her deceased husband's property.

This story and others like it in the Bible make unpleasant reading, and we wonder why they are there. No one questions their truth, Unfortunately, there is abundant evidence to support the picture they draw of primitive society. But how did stories like these ever come to form part of Scripture? There can only be one answer-because the Book of God is the Book of Life. If sin mars the purity of its pages it is because sin mars life, and the Book will not permit the fact to be cut out of the Divine Revelation, or out of our minds.

Joseph in Egypt

In Potiphar's House.

Read chapter 39:1-20

- Joseph prospers
- His master's wife
- Joseph's refusal
- The accusation

In Prison.

Read chapter 39;21 - 40:23

- Joseph in charge
- The cupbearer's dream
- The baker's dream

- Joseph interprets the dreams
- "Remember me"

Pharaoh's Dreams.

Read chapter 41

- The seven cows
- The seven heads of grain
- The cupbearer remembers Joseph
- "God will give Pharaoh the answer he desires."
- Seven years of abundance
- Seven years of famine
- Joseph's advice to Pharaoh
- Joseph in charge
- Joseph in Pharaoh's service
- Manasseh and Ephraim born
- Severe famine everywhere

Joseph's Brothers visit Egypt.

Read chapter 42

- Grain in Egypt
- Ten brothers
- "You are spies"
- Brothers in custody for three days
- Joseph's demand
- The brothers' guilt
- Silver in the sacks of grain
- Return to Canaan
- Jacob's reluctance to send Benjamin

Second Visit.

Read chapter 43

- Severe famine
- Send our brother along with us
- Judah's responsibility
- Gifts to take with them

- Joseph's welcome
- The brothers' fear
- Simeon restored
- Joseph is moved
- The meal

Filling the Sacks.

Read chapter 44

- Joseph's silver cup in the sack of the youngest brother
- On their way home
- The accusation
- Finding the cup
- "How can we prove our innocence?"
- Judah explains
- Jacob continues to believe that Joseph is dead

Note on Chapter 44.5: Divining cups were supposed to possess magical properties. Some of them had an inscription engraved inside which, it was believed, would render poison ineffective, and increase the health value of wine or water drunk from them. There is a trace of the same superstition in telling fortunes from tea-leaves.

The Reconciliation.

Read chapter 45

- Joseph makes himself known
- "It was to save lives that God sent me ahead of you."
- "It was not you, who sent me here, but God."
- To preserve a remnant
- You shall live in the region of Goshen
- Pharaoh's approval
- Gifts for Jacob

Note on 25:10 On the eastern border of the Delta of the Nile, and near to the frontier of Palestine. Not good corn land, but land affording excellent pasture and plentiful supplies of vegetables and fish.

48

Jacob Goes to Egypt.

Read chapter 46 to 47:12

- Sacrifice at Beersheba
- "I will go down to Egypt with you."
- Everyone to Egypt
- (Leah's children)
- Reuben
  - Hanok,Pallu, Hezron, Karmi
- Simeon
  - Jemuel, Jamin, Ohad, Jakin, Zohar, Shaul
- Levi
  - Gershon, Kohath, Merari
- Judah
  - Er, Onan, Shelah, Perez, Zerah
    - (Er and Onan had died in Canaan)
    - Sons of Perez: Hezron and Hamul
- Issachar
  - Tola, Puah, Jashub, Shimron
- Zebulun
  - Sered, Elon, Jahleel
- Dinah
- (33 in all)
- (Zilpah's children)
- Gad
  - Zephon, Haggi, Shuni, Ezbon, Eri, Arodi, Areli
- Asher
  - Imnah, Ishvah, Ishvi, Beriah, Serah (daughter)
    - sons of Beriah: Heber, Malkiel
- (16 in all)
- (Rachel's children)
- Joseph
  - Manasseh, Ephraim
- Benjamin
  - Bela, Beker, Ashbel, Gera, Naaman, Ehi, Rosh, Muppim, Huppim, Ard
- (14 in all)

- (Bilhah's children)
- Dan
  - Hushim
- Naphtali
  - Jahziel, Guni, Jezer, Shillem
- (7 in all)
- Joseph meets his father in Goshen
- Shepherds detestable to the Egyptians
- family presented to Pharaoh
- Jacob blesses Pharaoh
- In the best part of the land

Famine in Egypt.

Read chapter 47:12-31

- Joseph collects money in exchange for grain
- Food in exchange for livestock
- Food in exchange for land
- The priests receive an allotment of food
- Joseph issues seed.
  - One fifth of produce to be given to Pharaoh
- Jacob's request

Note. We cannot judge Joseph's policy by modern social standards

Note on 48:31. Some bible version record that Isaac leaned on his staff; others that he leaned on the bed's head. The original Hebrew word of four letters can mean either, depending on the placing of the vowels in the word. Vowels were not added till much later.

Manasseh and Ephraim.

Read chapter 48

- Joseph takes his sons to Jacob
- Jacob speaks of God's promise
- "Ephraim and Manasseh will be mine."
- "Bring them to me so I may bless them."
- Jacob's right hand on Ephraim's head
- The blessing

Even commonplace buildings, like barns and granaries, which are to be seen dotted about every landscape, catch our eye on the sacred page, as if to remind us that the message written there directly concerns those who live and work on the land, who know the country scene, and are familiar with the life of the country-side.

51

- Ephraim put ahead of Manasseh
- Prophecy that God will take Joseph back to the land of his fathers

Note on 48.12: By taking the two boys between his knees Jacob adopted them as his children, thus giving them the right to be two independent tribes.

Jacob blesses his sons.

Read chapter 49:1-28

- Reuben
  - turbulent as the waters you will no longer excel
- Simeon and Levi
  - cursed be their anger
- Judah
  - The scepter will not depart from Judah, nor the ruler's staff from between his feet, until he to whom it belongs shall come and the obedience of the nations shall be his
- Zebulun
  - will live by the seashore and become a haven for ships
- Issachar
  - will bend his shoulder to the burden and submit to forced labour
- Dan
  - will provide Justice for his people
  - will be a snake by the roadside
- Gad
  - will be attacked by raiders but he will attach them at their heels
- Asher
  - his food will be rich
- Naphtali is a doe set free that bears beautiful fawns
- Joseph is a fruitful vine
  - Archers attacked him
  - but his strong arms stayed limber
  - because of the Almighty who blesses you with

blessings of the skies above
- Let all these rest on the head of Joseph, on the brow of the prince among his brothers.
- Benjamin is a ravenous wolf
- All these are the twelve tribes of Israel

The Death and burial of Jacob.
Read chapter 49: 29 - 50:14

- Jacob's instructions for his burial
- Embalming and mourning
- Joseph's request to Pharaoh
- The funeral procession
- "The Egyptians are holding a solemn ceremony of mourning."
- Return to Egypt

Joseph and his brothers.
Read chapter 50:15-21

- The brothers' fear
- "Am I in the place of God?"
- "God intended it for good."

Death of Joseph.
Read chapter 50:22-26

- One hundred and ten years
- Prophecy that God will take them out of this land
- "Carry my bones up from this place."
- Placed in a coffin

Let's read

EXODUS

Containing

Revelation by the river

Revelation by the sea

Revelation in the wilderness

Revelation on the mountain

Sanctuary of the all-revealing God

Exodus

The Lord of All the Earth

GOD STARTS MANKIND ON THE TRACK OF ITS TRUE DESTINY AND THEN LEADS THE WAY

There would have been no Western Civilization, as we know it, if God had not led the Israelites out of Egypt, and given them a code of laws upon which they could shape their lives. It is impossible to estimate how much our modern world owes to the events described in this book. Our history begins with the liberation of these slaves; which means, it was begun by God, and to His creative grace we owe whatever order and freedom we enjoy.

On this day, the greatest of days in human history, a new era of creation dawned. He who made the world and brought the Natural Order into being, who fashioned the earth to His own design and set it in the firmament of stars, now turned to the making of mankind, to the building of the Human or Social Order, to the fashioning of man, not as a creature of earth, for that had already been done, but as a member of society, with a relationship to his fellows and to the everlasting God of truth and right.

In calling Israel, God called mankind. Israel was His point of contact, that race among the races which knew His voice. As it was in the family of Israel (Jacob) so it is in the family of nations; God chooses the one who best serves His will for bringing the whole human family into the knowledge and possession of its heavenly destiny. Israel's history is the revelation of this purpose, and also the beginning of its realization.

The Revelation by the River

Read Chapter 1

- Names of the children of Israel
- Fruitful and increased in number
- A new king to whom Joseph meant nothing
- Forced labour
- Kill the baby boys
- The midwives
- The king's order

God spoke to his people who lived by the Nile

The Birth of Moses.

Read chapter 2:1-10

- The Child Hidden
- The basket among the reeds
- Pharaoh's daughter and his nurse
- Moses is named

Moses Flees to Midian.

Read chapter 2:11-25

- Hard labour
- Killing the Egyptian
- "Who made you ruler and judge over us?"
- Moses flees
- At the well
- Marriage to Zipporah
  - His son Gershom _ "I have become a foreigner in a foreign land"
- God's concern for Israel

News of God

Remember, over 400 years separates Genesis from Exodus, and the God who had spoken to Abraham, Isaac, and Jacob, was now speaking to Moses. He was still living. Time had not changed Him. The Living

56

*God, it seemed, was ever-living. I AM is His name, the always present
God, not the I was, nor the I will be, but the God now, of every situation.
To people in Israel's position this was great news.*

Moses at the Burning Bush.

Read chapter 3

- At Horeb, the mountain of God
- Burning but not consumed
- "You are standing on holy ground"
- "I am sending you to Pharaoh"

In the Name of God

- "I am who I am"
- Moses' commission
- "I will stretch out my hand and strike the Egyptians."

*Note on 3:14 No one, not even the ablest scholar, is able to say
dogmatically how these words should be translated and interpreted. It
would serve no good purpose to give all the different renderings which
have been proposed. The Divine Name remains a mystery. The reading
we offer is that which the context seems to require – the God of this
revelation, of this book and human life, is not an old, nor a new god, but
the everlasting God, who desires to be known as today's God.*

*Note on 3:22 Possibly some of the slaves looked upon the projected
journey to Sinai as a pilgrimage to a religious festival, and fully intended
to return what they borrowed, when they came back. On the other
hand, it is not inconceivable that long-tortured and cruelly burdened
slaves, with imperfect knowledge of God, should look upon the occasion
as an opportunity to rob their persecutors.*

By the Power of God.

Read chapter 4:1-17

- Moses' staff
- His leprous hand

He is also the God of those who live on the Yangtze

- Water from the Nile
- Slow of speech and tongue
- Send someone else
- Moses' brother Aaron

To the Work of God.

Read chapter 4:18-30

- Leaving Jethro
- Warning to Pharaoh
  - Israel is my firstborn son
  - I will kill your firstborn son
- Zipporah circumcises her son
- Aaron joins Moses in the wilderness
- Meeting with the elders of the Israelites

"Set my people free", saith the Lord

Conferring divine right on human freedom

The Living God, who has, in Genesis, declared Himself to be the Sovereign Lord of Nature and the Nations of the world, here makes it known that He is the Ruler of History. Time and the destiny of man are in His hands, and to mankind He now unfolds His plan. He will create a grand and glorious Humanity, and to that end demands that men, as sons of God, shall be free.

And of those who live on the Hudson and every other river

Appeal to Pharaoh.

Read Chapter 5:1-21

- Let my people go
- Who is the Lord that I should obey him?
- Burdens increased
- No longer to supply straw
- "You have made us obnoxious to Pharaoh

Appeal to God.

Read chapter 5:22 -6:12

- Moses speaks with God
- Reminder of the covenant
- I will redeem you
- Israel's discouragement

The family record of Moses and Aaron.

Read chapter 6:13-26

- Heads of their families
  - Hanok, Pallu, Hezron, Karmi, the sons of Reuben
  - Jemuel, Jamin, Ohad, Jakin, Zohar, Shaul, the sons of Simeon
- The clans of Levi
  - Gershon
    - Libni, Shimei

- Kohath
  - Amram, Izhar, Hebron, Uzziel
- Merari
  - Mahli, Mushi
- Amram married Jochebed, his father's sister.
  - Aaron and Moses
- Izhar's sons were Korah, Nepheg, Zikri
- Uzziel's sons were Mishael, Elzaphan, Sithri
- Aaron's sons were Nadab, abihu, Eleazar, Ithamar.
- Korah's sons were Assir, Elkanah, Abiasaph
- Eleazar married a daughter of Putiel. Their son was Phinehas

Aaron to speak for Moses.

Read chapter 6:26 to 7:13

- Moses' doubt
- "Aaron will be your prophet."
- The Egyptians will know that I am the Lord
- Aaron's miraculous Rod

Note on 7:3 Did God harden Pharaoh's heart? Bear this in mind:- in those days, and even among primitive and simple people today, events, which could quite easily be naturally explained, are frequently attributed to God's action by the words, 'It is the Lord's doing'. Such people do not mean to dishonour God, but if they knew Him better they would perhaps be more careful nor to attribute to Him things which contradict his nature and character.

In Pharaoh's Court

The one simple fact which shines through this strange story is that God has no competitor, and His resources are infinite. Only up to a point can the wizards of Egypt go. The fight against God can only end one way.

Read chapter 7:14 to 11:10

The plagues: So much has been written about the composition of this narrative, so many explanations have been offered for the wonders described in it, and so many attempts have been made to identify the Pharaoh, that it might be profitable to inquire what the picture means. To the Israelites God was, before their eyes, in life and action, revealing Himself as their Champion. He was challenging Pharaoh on his own ground. He was making it clear to mankind, once and for all, that throughout all the earth He was supreme.

The first nine plagues.

Read chapter 7:14 -10:29

- River of Blood
- Frogs
- Gnats (lice
- Flies
    - Distinction between Egyptians and Israelites
- Pharaoh: "Sacrifice here in the land."
- "You must not go very far."
- An epidemic: Livestock diseased
    - "No animal belonging to the Israelites will die"
- Boils
- "I have raised you up, that I might show you my power."
- Hail
    - but not in the land of Goshen
- "You and your officials still do not fear the Lord God."
- "How long will you refuse to humble yourself before me?"
- "How long will this man be a snare to us?"
- "Only the men can go"
- Locusts
- Darkness that can be felt
- "Even your women and children can go, but leave your livestock
- "Get out of my sight. The day you see my face you will die

Death of Firstborn Announced.

Read chapter 11

- One more plague
- Every firstborn son in Egypt will die

In the Home of Slaves

Read chapter 12:1 to 13:16

From the Court of Pharaoh to the homes of slaves came the Leader of Mankind looking for those who had not hardened their hearts against Him. Where He finds people who have put their trust in Him, though they be simple folk in humble dwellings, He gives them a token of His love which, outside their doors, can hardly be believed.

The Passover Instituted.

Read chapter 12: 1-28

- A new calendar
- The lamb for each man's family
- A year-old, without defect
- Blood on sides and tops of doorframes
- Eat with bitter herbs and bread without yeast
- Eat in haste
- Passover Sign - the blood on the houses
- "I will pass over you
- A day to commemorate for generations
- Instructions for the festival
- Celebrate the Festival of unleavened bread
- Moses passes on the instructions to the elders
- The children will ask

Note on 12:27 We must pause for a moment at this point, because it was during a celebration of this festival that our Lord was crucified, and it has always been the faith of Christians that this association of events was more than coincidence. The Apostle Paul speaks of 'Christ

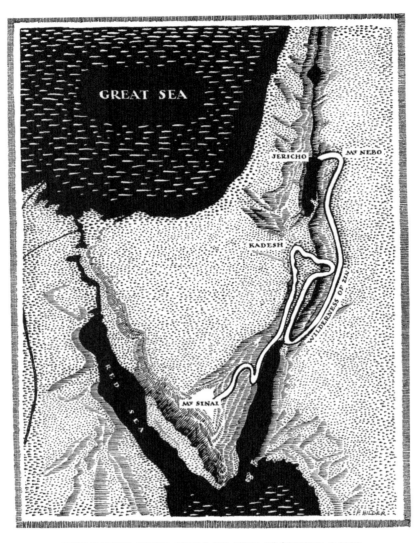

THE ROUTE FROM SINAI TO THE PROMISED LAND

Nothing remains to mark with certainty the places where the Israelites camped on their journey, except Sinai, and the identity of this mountain is not beyond question. We have followed the traditional route of the march and accepted the generally favoured situation of Sinai because there does not appear to be sufficient definite information to justify departure from them. Al alternative route takes a more easterly direction.

our Passover' (1 Corinthians. 5, 7), and our Lord Himself, when he sat at meat with His disciples at the Last Supper on the eve of the Passover, used words which justify the expression. He definitely linked His approaching death with the sacrifice which they, and all Israel, had come to Jerusalem to offer, though at the time the disciples did not realize they were about to see the Passover of their religion as the altar steps to a more amazing revelation.

For the Passover of the Exodus must be viewed not as an isolated incident in the history of Israel, but as the beginning of a progressive revelation which reached its fulfilment or completion in Christ. The Passover of Israel became the Passion of Redemption for all mankind, and the revelation which runs through the whole course of its development is nothing less than that of the fact and means of human salvation – of God's gracious way of enabling man to reach his divine destiny.

The point comes out clearly if we look at the setting of the revelation in the two Passover pictures already mentioned – the house with the blood-stained lintels, and the house with the upper room, How often the Bible turns our eyes towards homes, particularly to the homes of lowly people. Perhaps some day we shall discover that all the secrets of heaven are hidden in our homes. However, here are two homes, or rather two home scenes, one an out-of-door, and the other an in-door picture, each making its own contribution to the Passover revelation.

The first gives the idea of Divine Protection, and of deliverance from death. The second carries the thought to deliverance from sin, and passes on to the idea of Divine Provision for the growth, development, and perfecting of the spirit of man. God, who in one picture is watching over the homes of His people, in the other is with them in the home, guiding their thoughts and inspiring their fellowship. In a word, the God of the Passover is the God of our salvation, and this salvation is more than security from all our fears; it is access to a heavenly feast and communion in a heavenly fellowship.

The Passover Night.

Read chapter 12:29-30

- The tenth plague: Death of the Firstborn

The Exodus.

Read chapter 12:31-42

- Leave my people, you and the Israelites
- Silver and gold
- From Rameses to Sukkoth
- 430 years in Egypt

Passover Regulations

Read chapter 12:43-51

- No foreigner
- Inside the house
- Do not break any of the bones
- The whole community of Israel
- No uncircumcised male may eat it

The Firstborn Consecrated

Read chapter 13:1-2

- Consecrate to me every firstborn male
-

The Passover Story.

Read chapter 13:3-16

- Remember this day
- Observe this ceremony in the month of Aviv
- Unleavened bread for seven days
- Tell your son
  - This is what the Lord did for me when I came out of Egypt
- Keep this ordinance year after year
- All firstborn males of livestock belong to the Lord
- Redeem with a lamb every firstborn donkey
- When your son asks, "what does this mean?"
  - The Passover story

The Revelation by the Sea

Chapter 13:17 to 15:21

A leader must prove his ability to lead, and give evidence of his power to carry through his plans against unforeseen difficulties and overwhelming opposition. But has anyone, save God, ever brought His people so victoriously out of such a situation as faced Israel on the shores of the Red or Reedy Sea?

On the way to the sea.

Read chapter 13:17 - 14:9

- The Wilderness Way
- Joseph's bones
- Pillar of cloud and pillar of fire
- The camp by the sea
- The Egyptians will know that I am the Lord
- Pharaoh's change of mind
- The pursuit

Note on 13:21 If a natural explanation must be found for these beautiful symbols of God's guidance the most likely is that which says Sinai was at this time an active volcano. Its columns of smoke and fire could be seen for miles over the desert, and would be like a beacon signal given by the God of Sinai to those who were seeking their way to Him. There are obvious objections to this as to every other attempt to explain the mystery.

Pharaoh's Advancing Host.

Read chapter 14:10-31

- Israel's Fear
- Stand firm
- "Stretch out you hand over the sea."
- Darkness to the one side and light to the other side
- The waters divided
- Through the sea on dry land
- The Egyptian pursuit
- The water flowed back
- The lord saved Israel

Note on 14:30 The Lord saved Israel. To attempt to explain the matter in any other way, or go beyond the simple statements of the narrative seems unfitting, when the world today is full of the marvellous things men can do with so little knowledge of nature's forces.

Song of Deliverance

Read chapter 15:1-21

- I will sing to the Lord
- The Lord is my strength and my defence
- The Lord is a warrior
- Your right hand was majestic in power
- In the greatness of your majesty
- Who among the gods is like you?
- In your unfailing love you will lead the people you have redeemed
- The nations will hear and tremble
- The Lord reigns forever and ever
- Miriam's song

Great oceans, trackless, vast and wild, obey His Will

The Revelation in the Wilderness

Read Chapter 15:22 to 18:27

We strike the path of the onward march of humanity, God's company of slaves leading on, but we are more fortunate than they, for we know whither the way leads. Still, we need as they did, the help of Heaven to carry on, and it is not lacking.

Waters of Marah and Elim.

Read chapter 15:22-27

- Bitter waters made sweet
- The Lord's instruction
- I am the Lord, who heals you
- Wells of Elim

Note on 15:27 The God of the sea and the rivers is the God, too, of the wells and springs.

Manna and Quails.

Read chapter 16

- In the wilderness of Sin
- Grumbling against Moses and Aaron

- "I will rain down bread from Heaven
- The glory of the Lord appearing in the cloud
- Quail
- Manna. What is it?
- No one to keep any till morning
- Twice as much on the sixth day
- No manna on the Sabbath
- Manna with the tablets of the covenant law
- Manna for forty years

Note on 16:13 Quails, or partridges, in the early months of the year, fly in great numbers over this desert waste, and are often so exhausted that they are easily caught.

16:15 There is a shrub in the Sinai peninsula which, in the early summer, exudes heavy drops of sap or gum with a honey-like flavour, and it has been suggested that this might be the manna of the story. The Arabs speak of it by this name. It is, however, found only in small quantities, and quickly disappears under the heat of the sun.

A Hidden Spring: water from the rock.

Read chapter 17:1-7

- Camp at Rephidim
- Thirsty for water
- Strike the rock and water will come out of it
- Massah and Meribah: Is the Lord among us or not?

A Vain Attack; Victory over the Amalekites.

Read chapter 17:8-15

- Attacked by the Amalekites
- Moses at the top of the hill
- Joshua fought
- Aaron and Hur hold up Moses' hands
- I will completely blot out the name of Amalek
- The Lord is my banner

A Family Reunion; Jethro's Advice.

Read Chapter 18

- Camp near the mountain of God
- Moses meets with Jethro
- A burnt offering
- Moses takes his seat as judge
- "Why do you alone sit as judge?"
- Select capable men"
- Advice heeded

Note on 18:21 Men of ability and character. Jethro counselled the delegation of responsibility – a principle which has many advocates today.

The Revelation on the Mountain

Read chapter 19:1 to 34:35

And yet it would be a mistake to think of this Divine Revelation as nothing more than a code of laws and regulations to be formally observed. These laws are but the scaffolding of a Divine Humanity which one day will be the Temple of the Living God. They are the framework within which the creative powers of God and man, working together, will build the new Jerusalem or City of God. Within the laws it is not difficult to see the foundations which God has laid down, nor the lines on which He wants man's work to proceed.

At Mount Sinai.

Read chapter 19

- Israel camped at Mount Sinai
- If you obey me fully and keep my covenant
- You will be my treasured possession
- A kingdom of priests and a holy nation
- The elders' response
- Be ready by the third day
- Limits round the mountain

Sinai, a desert mountain, is crowned with glory

- Mountain covered with smoke
- Moses spoke and the voice of God answered him
- bring Aaron up with you

The Ten Commandments.

Read chapter 20:1-21

- No other gods
- No graven image
- Do not misuse the name of the Lord
- Keep the Sabbath day holy
- Honour your father and your mother
- You shall not murder
- You shall not commit adultery
- You shall not steal
- You shall not give false testimony
- You shall not covet
- Trembling with fear
- Moses tells the people not to fear

Until the twentieth century no one denied the rightness of the second half of the Commandments. But our age has seen a revolt against authority, and against all moral codes of conduct, with the result that the social and moral orders have been thrown into chaos and confusion and these long-standing laws of God which built up our history have been severely questioned. However, they have not yet been destroyed and their voice is still imperative. When they are translated into terms which show their universal and abiding character — the sacredness of life, the purity of home life, the property of others, etc. – their need is still urgent.

The first half of the code we seem to have lost or forgotten completely, and yet it is more vital, because it is related to the highest region of human experience. We think little of worship, but: it is the native air and country of man's creative spirit. Few realize it, and it may not be until we reach the age of Leisure to which history is taking us, that the full meaning and value of worship will become clear, and make manifest the glorious wisdom of our God.

The Judgments:

chapter 20:22 to 24:18

Before the altar of God, which stands at the head of this chapter like a sacred symbol in a Court of Law, human rights and liberties are invested with a new dignity, and whatever a man does has to be judged in the light of this new revelation.

Altar for the Open Court:
The Law of the Altar.
Read chapter 20:22-26

- Do not make gods of silver or gold
- An altar of earth
- Wherever I cause my name to be honoured,
  - I will come to you and bless you

Justice for slaves.

Read chapter 21:1-11

- Set free in the seventh year
- If servant desires to continue to serve his master
  - Pierce his ear with an awl
- Daughter as a servant

Note on 21:1 Hypothetical cases for the guidance of judges. It is interesting to notice that there was no punishment by imprisonment, though in Joseph's time there were prisons. There was no torture. The form of punishment was in the form of restitution, or even retaliation, but this was well regulated and evidently supervised by judges. In an age when revenge might run to extremes, the law of retaliation prescribed limits.

Note on 21:6 Probably because of the obvious connection between 'hearing' and 'obeying'.

Capital Offences.

Read chapter 21: 12-17

- Death for murder
- Place to flee to for unintentional killing
- Attacking father or mother
- Kidnapping
- Cursing father or mother

Compensation Acts.

Read chapter 21: 18-32

- Striking with stone or fist
  - Payment for healing
- Beating a slave with a rod
  - Punished if death occurs
- Hitting a pregnant woman

- fined if no serious injury
- If serious injury
  - life for life, eye for eye, tooth for tooth, hand for hand, foot for foot, burn for burn, wound for wound, bruise for bruise
- Destroying the eye of a slave
  - freedom for slave
- Knocking out a tooth of a slave
  - freedom for slave
- If an ox gores a person to death
  - Death for ox and its meat not eaten
- If ox had the habit of goring and not penned up by the owner
  - Both ox and owner to be put to death
  - Owner may redeem his life by payment
- If ox gores a male or female slave
  - Pay thirty shekels of silver to the master

Injuries to cattle.

Read chapter 21:33-36

- Animal falling into a pit
  - Pay owner for the loss
- Ox killing an ox
  - Sell the live ox and divide the money equally
- If ox had the habit of goring and not penned up by the owner
  - Owner must pay

Theft or Damage.

Read chapter 22;1-

- Stealing an ox or sheep
  - Pay back 5 cattle for cattle or 4 sheep for sheep
- Catching a thief at night
  - Not guilty of bloodshed
- If after sunrise

- Guilty of bloodshed
- Restitution for stealing
- Straying livestock
- In case of fire

Breaches of Trust.

Read chapter 22:1-15

- Goods left for safekeeping
- Cases of illegal possession to be brought before judges
- Death of an animal left for safekeeping
- Injury or death of a borrowed animal

Social Responsiblity.

Read chapter 22:16-31

- Bride price for seducing a virgin
- Do not allow a sorceress to live
- Death for anyone who lies with an animal
- Destruction for anyone who sacrifices to any god but the Lord
- Do not mistreat a foreigner
- Do not take advantage of a widow or fatherless
- Charge no interest if you lend money to the needy
- Do not blaspheme God
- Do not hold back offerings
- Give the firstborns to the Lord
- Do not eat the meat of an animal torn by wild beasts

Note on 22:18 Witchcraft is no longer practised in our country, and witches, if there are any, would not now be put to death. These early laws or judgments must be interpreted and applied in the light of the Christian revelation. The permanent truth behind this law is that magic must not be allowed to have any place in religion.

Falsehood and Revenge.

Read chapter 23:1-9

- Do not spread false reports
- Do not follow the crowd in doing wrong
- Return a wandering ox or donkey
- Do not deny justice to the poor
- Do not accept a bribe
- Do not oppress a foreigner

Sabbaths and Festivals.

Read chapter 23:10-19

- Sow and harvest for six year
- Leave the land unploughed the seventh year
- Six days work, seventh day rest
- Three annual festivals
  - Festival of Unleavened Bread
  - Festival of Harvest, firstfruits of the crops
  - Festival of ingathering
- Do not offer blood of a sacrifice with anything containing yeast
- Bring the best to the house of the Lord
- Do not cook a young goat in its mother's milk.

The Angel of the Lord.

Read chapter 23:20-33

- My angel to guard you
- My name is in him
- Worship the Lord your God and his blessing will be on your food and water
- I will send my terror ahead of you
- I will send the hornet ahead of you
- Little by little
- I will establish your borders
- Do not make a covenant with them or their gods
- The worship of their gods will be a snare to you

Note on 23:20 The word does not necessarily mean a supernatural

Sinai's glory hallows all mountain solitudes

being. It signifies a messenger, and there is no strong objection to applying the word to Moses. A person is denoted, and in his nearness to God and his service for God Moses fulfilled the ministry of an angel. 'My name is in him' means: he has my authority.

The seventy Elders.
Read chapter 24: 1-4

- Moses alone to approach the Lord
- "Everything the Lord has said we will do."

Blood Bond.
Read chapter 24:4-11

- Twelve stone pillars
- Offerings made
- Half the blood in basins; half sprinkled on the altar
- The book of the covenant
- Blood sprinkled on the people
- The blood of the covenant

- Pavement of lapis lazuli (Sapphire stone)
- The seventy elders saw Gopd and ate and drank

Note on 24:6 We do not need to go into the details of primitive customs to understand the binding nature of a bond ratified by blood sprinkling. Human nature instinctively feels a sense of awe and seriousness at the sight of blood.

The Glory of the Lord.

Read 24:12-18

- Tablets of stone
- The law and commandments
- The mountain of God
- Glory of God settled on Mount Sinai
- Like a consuming fire
- Moses on the mountain forty days and nights

The Tabernacle

Exodus 25:1-38:18

Why this long description of the Tabernacle, and, after a short break dealing with a lapse into idolatry, another almost identical description of the same building? Surely, that we shall not miss nor undervalue the importance of worship to the new Humanity.

Offerings for the Tabernacle.

Read 25:1-9

- An offering from everyone, whose heart prompt them to give
- Have them make a sanctuary for me

The Ark and Table.

Read chapter 25:10-30

- An ark of acacia wood

- Poles to carry it
- Tablets of the covenant law in the ark
- Atonement cover of pure gold
- Two cherubim
- Wings spread upwards, covering the mercy seat
- "I will meet with you and give you all my commands
- Table of acacia wood
- Four gold ringsfasten to the four corners
- Poles overlayed with gold
- Plates and dishes of pure gold
- Bread of the Presence on the table at all times

Note on 25:10 A chest of acacia wood, 3 ft. 9 in. long, 2 ft. 3 in. wide, and 2 ft. 3 in. deep. The most important article in the Holy of Holies. It contained the Tables of the Law which, to Israel, were the sacred tokens of the Covenant. A slab of pure gold, called the Mercy Seat, and decorated with symbolic figures, covered the Ark. According to Babylonian analogy the figures typified 'guardians'.

The Golden Candlestick.

Read 25:31-40

- Lampstand of pure gold
- Six branches, three on each side
- Seven lamps

Framework and Covering.

Read chapter 26:1-37

- Ten Curtains of finely twisted linen
- 28 cubits long and 4 cubits wide
- Join five curtains together. Joinnthe other five together
- 50 gold clasps to fasten curtains
- The tabernacle is a unit
- 11 curtains of goat hair for the tent over the tabernacle
- 50 loops and 50 Bronze clasps
- Fasten the tent together as a unit
- A covering of ram skins dyed red

- Covering of durable leather
- Upright frames
- Twenty frames for the south side
- Twenty frames for the north side
- Six frames for the west side and two frames for the corners
- Crossbars of acacia wood
- Centre cross bar to extend from end to end at the middle of the frame
- Overlay with gold
- Curtain of blue, purple and scarlet yarn and finely twisted linen
- Ark of covenant law behind the curtain
- Curtain to separate the Holy Place from the Most Holy Place
- Table outside the curtain on north side
- Lampstand on the south side
- Curtain for the entrance

The Altar of Burnt offering.

Read chapter 27:1-8

- Altar of acacia wood three cubits high, five cubits long, five cubits wide
- Horn at each corn er
- Utensils of bronze
- Poles of acacia wood, overlaid with bronze

The Court of the Tabernacle.

Read chapter 27:8-19

- South side 100 cubits long, twenty posts
- North side 100 cubits
- West end 50 cubits, ten posts
- East end 50 cubits, ten posts
- Curtains, 15 cubits long, on one side; curtains 15 cubits long on other side
- Curtain 20 cubits long for the entrance

- Articles in service of the tabernacle to be of bronze

Oil for the lampstand.

Read chapter 27:20-21

- Clear oil of pressed olives
- Lamps to be kept burning from evening till morning
- A lasting ordinance

Garments for the Priesthood.

Read chapter 28:1-30

- Aaron and his sons to minister as Priest
- Garments to make
  - a breastpiece
  - an ephod
  - a robe
  - a woven tunic
  - a turban
  - a sash
- The Ephod of gold and blue, purple and scarlet yarn
  - Two shoulder pieces
  - Two onyx stones engraved withnames of the sons of Israel
  - Aaron to bear the names on his shoulders
- The Breastplate of gold and blue, purple and scarlet yarn
  - Four rows of precious stones
  - Twelve stones
  - Braided chains of pure gold
  - Two gold rings
  - Attached to the ephod
- Aaron to bear the names of the sons of Israel over his heart
- Urim and Thummim in the breastplate
  - The means of making decisions

Note on 28:6 Possibly some kind of garment covering the chest and back and supported by shoulder-straps. It was made of the same material as the Tabernacle fabrics to suggest the close relationship between the Priests and the Sanctuary.

Note on 28:29 Like a silent prayer the jewels shine, bearing the name of each family to God.

Other priestly garments.

Read chapter 28:31-43

- The robe of the ephod of blue cloth
  - Pomegranates of blue, purple and scarlet yarn around the hem
  - Bells of Gold
- A plate of pure Gold: HOLINESS TO THE LORD
  - Attached to the Turban
- It will be on Aaron's forehead
- He will bear the guilt involved in the sacred gifts
- Tunic and turban of fine linen
- Tunics, sashes and caps for Aaron's sons
- Linen undergarments
- Aaron and his sons to wear them whenever they enter the tent of meeting

Note on 28:33 So that the people should know when the High Priest entered the Holy Place and they should devote themselves to prayer

Consecration of Priests.

Read chapter 29

- Young bull, two rams, round loaves without yeast.
- Bring Aaron to the door of the tabernacle
- Anointing oil
- Slaughter the bull
  - Blood on the horns of the altar
  - Internal organs burnt on the altar
  - Hide bull's flesh, hide and intestines outside the camp
  - A sin offering
- Slaughter one of the rams
  - Blood on the sides of the altar

- Burn on the altar
- A burnt offering
- Slaughter the other ram
- Blood on the right ears of Aaron and his sons,
  - on the thumbs of their right hands
  - in the big toe of their right feet
- Blood from the altar and anointing oil
  - Sprinkle on Aaron and his garments
  - Sprinkle on Aaron's sons and their garments
- The fat from this ram, one thick loaf with olive oil, one thin loaf
  - Place in the hands of Aaron and his sons
  - Wave them before the Lord
  - A wave offering
  - Then burn them on the altar
- The perpetual share for Aaron and his sons
- Aaron's sacred garments will belong to his descendants
- Aaron and his sons to eat the meat of the ram and the bread
  - No on else to eat them
- Sacrifice a bull each day for seven days as a sin offering
- Offer each day two rams, one in the morning and one at twilight
- At the door of the tabernacle
  - I will meet you and speak to you
  - I will dwell among the Israelites and be their god

The Altar of Incense.

Read chapter 30:1-5
- Altar of acacia wood for burning incense
- A cubit long and a cubit wide, two cubits high
- Poles of acacia wood to carry it
- Place it in front of the curtain
- Burn incense every morning and at twilight
- Once a year Aaron shall make atonement on its horns

Redemption Tax (Atonement money).

Read chapter 30:11-16

- At every census
  - Each one must pay a ransom for his life
- Half shekel is an offering to the Lord
- All who are over twenty
- Rich not to give more
- Poor not to give less
- Use it for the service of the Tabernacle

The Bronze Laver (Basin for washing).

Read chapter 30:17-21

- Between the tent of meeting and the altar
- Wash hands and feet
- Aaron and his descendants

The Holy Anointing Oil.

Read chapter 30:22-33

- Fine spices
  - 500 shekels of liquid myrrh
  - 250 shekels of cinnamon
  - 250 shekels of sweet calamus
  - 500 shekels of cassia
  - A hin of olive oil
- Make into a sacred anointing oil to anoint
  - the tent of meeting
  - the ark of the covenant law
  - the table and all its articles
  - the lampstand and its accessories
  - the basin
- Anoint Aaron and his sons
- Do not pour it on anyone else

The Incense.

Read chapter 30:34-38

- Fragrant spices
  - gum resin, onycha, galbanum and pure frankincense (equal amounts)
- to be salted and pure and sacred
- Grind some to powder and place in front of the ark of the covenant law
- Do not make incense with this formula for yourselves

Inspired Craftsmen.

Read chapter 31:1-11

- Bezalel - filled with the Spirit of God
  - to make artistic designs
- Oholiab to help him
- "I have given ability to all skilled workers."

The Sabbath.

Read chapter 31:12-18

- "Observe the Sabbath, because it is holy to you."
  - Those who work must be cut off from their people
  - Whoever does any work is to be put to death
  - Celebrate it for generations to come
- Two tablets of covenant law
-
-

Worship:

Read chapters 32:1 to 34:35

Between two pictures of the Tabernacle we are shown a very different kind of worship. However, the golden idol is ground to dust, the broken laws are renewed, and the goodness of the Lord makes the worship of Him a glorious service. We are given a revelation of His character which has become the keynote of His worship throughout the world.

Voice of the People; The Gold Calf.

Read chapter 32:1-6

- "Make us gods who will go before us."
- An idol cast in the shape of a calf
  - "These are your gods."
- Indulging in revelry

The Voice of God.

Read chapter 32:7-14

- "They are a stiff-necked people."
  - 'Leave me alone that I might destroy them
- Moses pleads for the people
  - Turn from your fierce anger
  - Remember your servants Abraham, Isaac and Israel
- The Lord relented

Note on 32:8 Idolatry has to be seen as the forsaking of the true and only God, if its real character is to be fully estimated. The substitution of helpless and worthless idols as objects of worship is, to modern readers, ignorant foolishness, which no intelligent person or community would in these days commit, but to throw over God, for no god at all, as many moderns do, is surely a greater sin.

The Writing of God.

Read chapter 32:15-35

- Two tablets of the covenant law
- "The sound of war in the camp"
- Tablets broken at the foot of the mountain
- The calf burned in the fire
  - Ground to powder, scattered on the water
  - Israelites made to drink it
- Aaron's explanation
  - I threw the gold into the fire and out came this calf
- "Who is on the Lord's side, let him come to me"
- Levites rallied to Moses
  - Three thousand of the people died

PASSING ON THE REVELATION TO THE PRESENT AGE

One of the first books to be printed was the Bible, and there is no finer testimony to the perpetual value of the Divine Revelation than the constant stream of new editions which has issued from the printing presses from that day to this.

- Forgive their sin — but if not, then blot me out of the book you have written
- "Whoever has sinned against me I will blot out of my book"
- The people struck with a plague

The Command to Leave Sinai:

Read chapter 33

- I will send an angel before you
- But I will not go with you
- The people mourned
- Israelites stripped off their ornaments

The tabernacle of God (Tent of meeting)

- Outside the camp
- Pillar of cloud
- The Lord spoke to Moses face to face, as one speaks to a friend
- His servant Joshua
- "My presence will go with you"
- "Show me your glory."
- "I will have mercy on whom I will have mercy, and I will have compassion on whom I will have compassion."
- A cleft in the rock

The Goodness of God.

Read chapter 34:1-9

- Moses makes new Tablets
- The LORD, the LORD, the compassionate and gracious God, slow to anger, abounding in love and faithfulness, maintaining love to thousands, and forgiving wickedness, rebellion and sin.

Note on 34:6 God's true glory is His goodness. It is inward, ethical, and displayed in His character. This is a marvellous passage. The revelation we are asked to contemplate is not the glory of His infinity or eternity, but His everlasting mercy and boundless compassion.

The Covenant of God.

Read chapter 34:10-17

- Before all your people I will do wonders
- Be careful not to make a treaty with those who live in the land
- Break down their altars
- Do not worship any other god

The God of the Passover.

Read chapter 34: 18-26

- Celebrate the Festival of unleavened bread
- The first offspring of every womb belongs to me
- Redeem all your firstborn sons
- On the seventh day you shall rest
- The festival of Weeks
- The Festival of Ingathering
- Men to appear before the Lord three times a year
- Do not offer the blood of the sacrifice with anything containing yeast

Note on 34:18,21 The references to the Sabbath, the Festivals, and the Sacrifices, strike the note of the times for worship throughout the year. Between the pictures of the Sanctuary we hear the Church Bells.

The Radiance of God.

Read chapter 34:27-35

- Moses with the Lord forty days and forty nights
- The ten commandments
- Moses' radiant face
- Veil over Moses' face

Sanctuary of the All-Revealing God

Building and Furnishing the Tabernacle:

Read Chapters 35 to 40

At this Sanctuary history lingers. The journey is not resumed until Leviticus has made us acquainted with the movement which was born and cradled in this, the first true House of God. But that story cannot be told until the House is built; so here we are shown the builders at work, and the quality of their workmanship.

Sabbath Regulations and Offerings for the Tabernacle.

Read chapter 35:1-19

- Everyone who is willing
  - bring an offering

- All who are skilled
  - Come and make everything the Lord has commanded
    - The tabernacle
    - The ark
    - The table
    - The lampstand
    - The altar of incense
    - The curtain
    - The altar of burnt offering
    - The bronze basin
    - The curtains of the courtyard
    - The curtain for the entrance
    - The tent pegs and their ropes
    - The woven garments

The Great Offertory.

Read chapter 35:20-29

- Everyone who was willing brought an offering
  - Gold as a wave offering
  - Blue, purple or scarlet yarn
  - Durable leather
  - Silver or bronze
- Every skilled woman spun
- Leaders brought onyx stones and other gems
  - Spices and olive oil
  - freewill offerings

God's Workmen. Bezalel and Oholiab.

Read chapter 35:30 -36:7

- Bezalel filled with the Spirit of God
- Oholiab to teach others
- All kinds of work
- Received from Moses all the offerings
- More than enough

The Tabernacle.
Read chapter 36:8-38

- The curtains
- The upright frames of acacia wood
- The crossbars of acacia wood
- Four posts of acacia wood
- Curtain for the entrance and five posts with hooks

The Ark.
Read chapter 37:1-9

- Bezalel made the ark of acacia wood
- Poles to carry it
- Atonement cover (Mercy Seat) of pure gold
- Two cherubim

The Table.
Read chapter 37:10-16

- Table of acacia wood
- Gold rim
- Four gold rings to hold the poles
- Articles of pure gold
    - Plates, dishes, bowls, pitchers

Note on 37:10 On this Table of Shew-bread – bread set out or exhibited – stood the golden dishes which held the flat cakes of bread made each week for the offering, with the flagons and chalices for the wine. Its place is taken in the Christian Church by the Holy Table.

Note on 37:16 These spoons or pans were for holding the frankincense, and were placed, one on each of the two piles of bread. All the gifts on this Table were in the nature of a continual thank-offering to God for His daily bounty, and an acknowledgement that they were to be used in His service.

The Lampstand.

Read chapter 37:17-24

- Pure gold
- Six branches
- Three cups shaped like almond flowers on each side
- Four cups shaped like almond flowers with buds and blossoms
- All of one piece hammered out of pure gold
- Seven lamps of pure gold

The Altar of Incense.

Read chapter 37:25-28

- Acacia wood
- Top, sides and horns overlaid with pure gold
- Gold rings to hold the poles to carry it
- Poles of acacia wood
- Sacred anointing oil

The Altar of Burnt Offering.

Read chapter 38:1-7

- Acacia wood
- A horn at each of the four corners
- Overlaid with bronze
- Utensils of bronze
- A Grating for the altar
- Bronze rings to hold the poles for the four corners of the bronze grating

The cathedrals we are building now show how the Tent Sanctuary has been enriched by the ages. Originally the Tabernacle must have been little more than a tent set apart for waiting upon God, but it set the pattern of the House of God for all time.

The Laver (Basin for washing).

Read chapter 38:8

- Bronze basin and stand made from mirrors of the women

Note on 38:8. At the entrance to some of the heathen temples it was customary to have mirrors of burnished brass for the women who were taking part in the pagan services. In the tabernacle these idolatrous practices are abolished.

The Outer Court.

Read chapter 38: 9-20

- South side a hundred cubits long
- Curtains of finely twisted linen
- North side also a hundred cubits long
- West side fifty cubits wide
- East end towards the sunrise fifty cubits wide
- Curtains
- Bases for posts were bronze
- Curtain for the entrance of blue, purple and scarlet yarn and fine linen
- Tent pegs of bronze

Gold and Silver Work.

Read chapter 38:21-30

- Total amount of gold
  - 29 talents and 730 shekels
- Silver
  - 100 talents and 1775 shekels
- 603,550 men 20 years old or more
- bronze
  - 70 talents and 2400 shekels

The Priestly Garments.

Read chapter 39: 1-31

- The Breastplate of gold and of blue, purple and scarlet yarn
- Four rows of precious stones
- Twelve stones, engraved with names of twelve tribes
- Braided chains of gold and gold rings
- The Ephod Cassock entirely of blue cloth
- Pomegranates of blue, purple and scarlet yarn
- Bells of pure gold
- Tunics of fine linen
- Turban of fine linen
- Linen caps
- Linen undergarments
- Sash of fine linen
- Plate of the holy crown of pure gold
- Engraved with "HOLINESS TO THE LORD"

Note on 39:30 *The great words reveal the purpose and promise of God for the new humanity which, beginning with Israel, He has set out to create. Until we discover what the call means, for a Divine Call it is, and see it not as an end in itself but as an initial step, a preparation for new creative work with, and service for, God, we shall never enter into the glorious inheritance which God has prepared for mankind.*

Moses inspects the Tabernacle.

Read chapter 39:32-42

- Israelites did everything as the Lord commanded Moses
- They brought the tabernacle to Moses
- Moses blessed them

The Tabernacle erected and arranged:

Read chapter 40:1-33

- Set up the Tabernacle on the first day of the first month
  - The Ark
  - The table
  - The lampstand
  - The altar of incense
  - The altar of burnt offering
  - The basin
  - The courtyard
- Anoint the tabernacle and everything in it
- Bring Aaron and his sons and wash them
- Anoint him and his sons
  - Their anointing will be to a priesthood that will continue throughout their generations
- Tablets of the law placed in the ark
- The ark brought into the tabernacle and the shielding curtain hung
- The table placed in the tent of meeting
- The lampstand opposite the table
- The gold altar in the tent of meeting in front of the curtain
- The altar of burnt offering near the entrance
- The basin between the tent of meeting and the altar

The Crowning Glory.

Read chapter 40:34-38

- The glory of the Lord filled the tabernacle
- Whenever the cloud lifted from above the tabernacle the Israelites would set out
- Cloud over the tabernacle by day
- Fire was in the cloud by night.

Printed in Great Britain
by Amazon

29021551R00059